This book is dedicated to :

__HPJC     children__
(Name of Child)

May your smile and glow light up the world like the sun!

Copyright © 2021 by Dr. Pamela Gurley

All Rights Reserved.

No part of this publication may be reproduced, distributed, or transmitted in any form or by any means, including photocopying, recording, or other electronic or mechanical methods, without the prior written permission of the publisher, except in the case of brief quotations embodied in a book review and certain other noncommercial uses permitted by copyright law.

For permission requests, send an email to: admin@clarkandhillenterprise.com

First Printing

ISBN Hardcover: 978-1-7342218-5-5

ISBN E-Book: 978-1-7342218-6-2

Printed in the United States of America

Clark and Hill Enterprise, LLC

6655 Santa Barbara Rd, #8681

Elkridge, MD 21075

www.clarkandhillenterprise.com

www.iamdrpgurley.com

# Brown Girl, Be SOCIAL

When you wake up in the morning, Brown Girl,
Be EXCITED.

Dare to let your curls twist, turn, bend, and bounce.

Mix prints and stripes with colors that are bold and bright.

And when you look in the mirror, Brown Girl, Be CONFIDENT.

Your eyes, your nose,
and your lips
were painted perfectly
on your beautiful face.

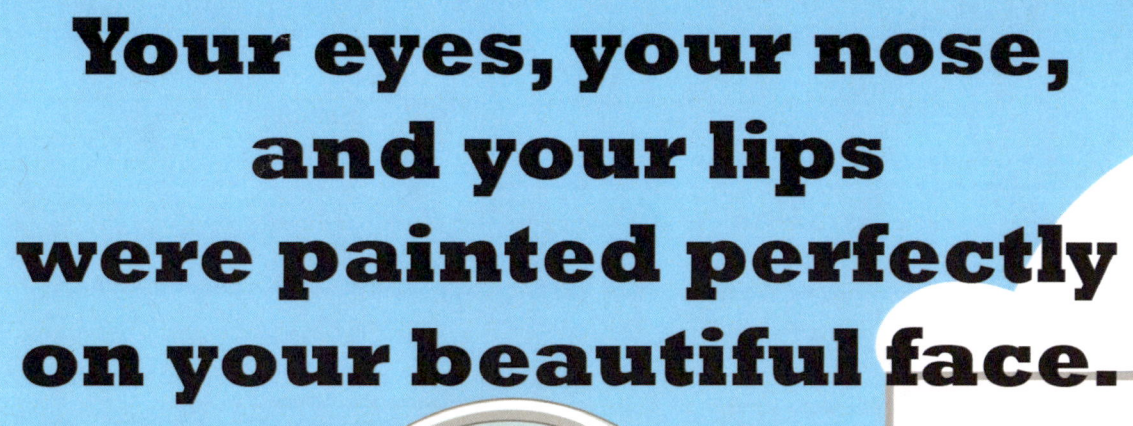

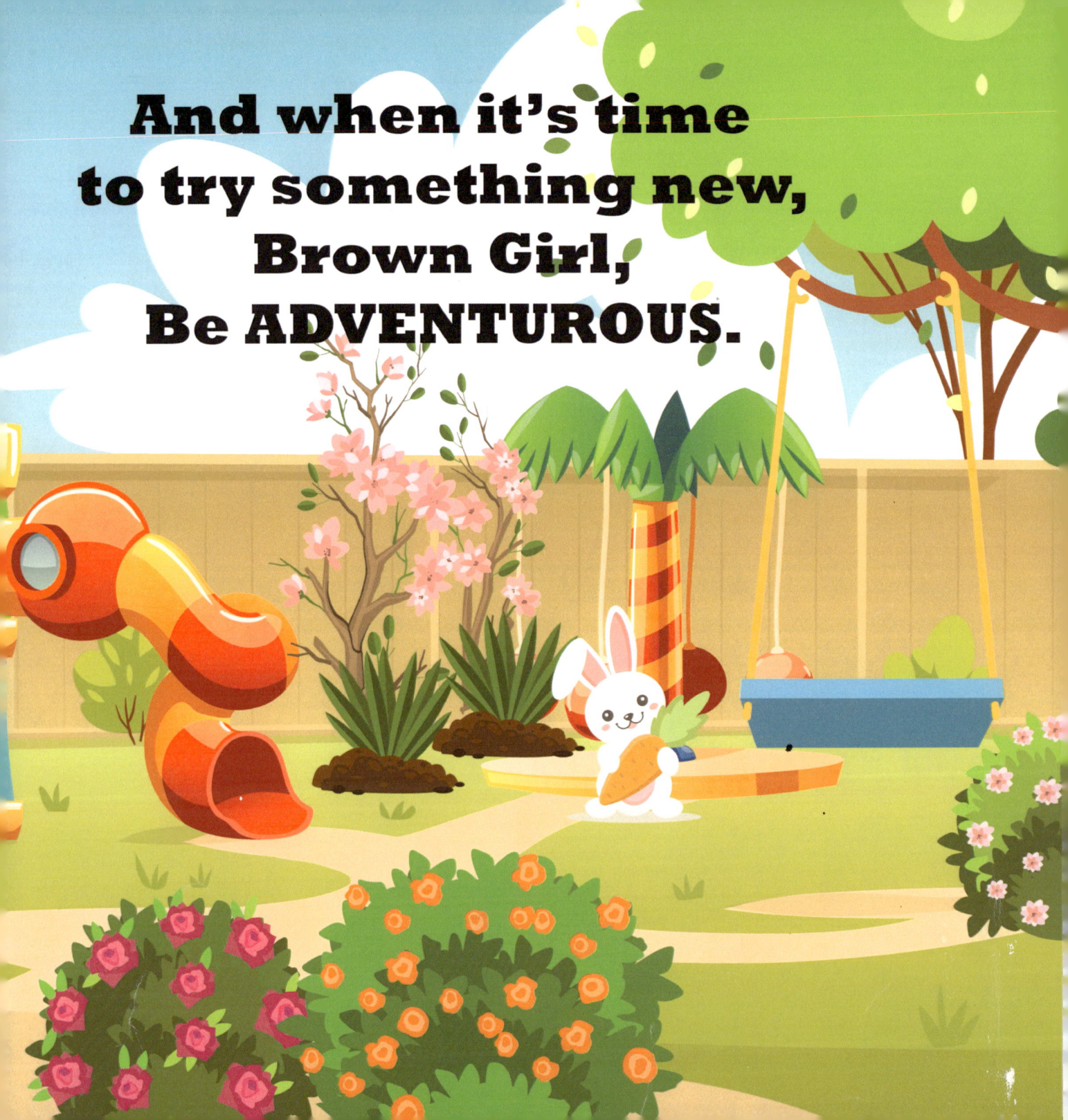

And when you face something tough, Brown Girl, Be BRAVE.

You can do anything and everything you set your mind to do.

Let your warm smile and white teeth beam and shine .

Of the brown skin you're in.
It is part of your legacy.

Just say hello and tell them your name.

Because anyone would be lucky to know an

## About the Author

Professional Speaker and Author, Dr. Pamela Gurley is the founder and CEO/Founder of @clarkandHillEnterprise, CEO/Founder of IamDrPGurley; CEO/Founder of Un@apologeticbyDrG (@unapologeticbydrg), CEO/Founder of D.A.W. Entertainment, Contributing Author of "Living A Non-Negotiable Lifestyle: My Life + My Dream + My Ambition = My Success"; Adjunct Graduate School Professor; Founder and Host of Herspiration Happy Hour podcast; Host of Vlog Series Un@pologetic w/ DrG; Editor/Contributing Writer for We Empower (WE) and Hustle & Soul Magazine.

Dr. Pam has been featured in Forbes and Hype Magazine; as well as, on Good Morning Washington (abcDC7), Good Day Atlanta (Fox5Atl), The Quiet Storm w/ Lenny Green, The Book of Sean (FoxSoul), Hot914 Radio, Fox34, NBC, CBS, and many other media outlets.

She is a retired United States Army Veteran and holds a Bachelor of Arts in Psychology from Saint Leo University; a Master's in Health Service Administration from Central Michigan University; and a Doctorate in Management with a concentration in Organizational Development and Change from Colorado Technical University.

## Other books by author

1. I am Not a Stereotype: I Am H.E.R.
2. Bl@ck Girl Activist
3. Brown Boy Be Social

CPSIA information can be obtained
at www.ICGtesting.com
Printed in the USA
LVRC081334260721
693698LV00008B/229